ISSUES AND ANSWERS *Collection*

The
BENEFIT *of*
the DOUBT

Encouragement for the Questioning Christian

CHARLES R. SWINDOLL

INSIGHT FOR LIVING

The Benefit of the Doubt: Encouragement for the Questioning Christian
An Issues and Answers Collection Book

From the Bible-Teaching Ministry of Charles R. Swindoll

Charles R. Swindoll has devoted his life to the clear, practical teaching and application of God's Word and His grace. A pastor at heart, Chuck has served as senior pastor to congregations in Texas, Massachusetts, and California. He currently pastors Stonebriar Community Church in Frisco, Texas, but Chuck's listening audience extends far beyond a local church body. As a leading program in Christian broadcasting, *Insight for Living* airs in major Christian radio markets around the world, reaching people groups in languages they can understand. Chuck's extensive writing ministry has also served the body of Christ worldwide and his leadership as president and now chancellor of Dallas Theological Seminary has helped prepare and equip a new generation for ministry. Chuck and Cynthia, his partner in life and ministry, have four grown children and ten grandchildren.

Published by IFL Publishing House, A Division of Insight for Living
Post Office Box 251007, Plano, Texas 75025-1007

Editor in Chief: Cynthia Swindoll, President, Insight for Living
Executive Vice President: Wayne Stiles, Th.M., D.Min., Dallas Theological Seminary
General Editor: Derrick G. Jeter, Th.M., Dallas Theological Seminary
Theological Editor: John Adair, Th.M., Ph.D., Dallas Theological Seminary
Content Editor: Amy L. Snedaker, B.A., English, Rhodes College
Copy Editors: Jim Craft, M.A., English, Mississippi College
   Kathryn Merritt, M.A., English, Hardin-Simmons University
Project Coordinator/Editor, Creative Ministries: Melanie Munnell, M.A., Humanities,
   The University of Texas at Dallas
Project Coordinator, Communications: Nancy Holmes, A.A.S. Eastern New Mexico University – Roswell
Proofreader: Paula McCoy, B.A., English, Texas A&M University-Commerce
Designer: Laura Dubroc, B.F.A., Advertising Design, University of Louisiana at Lafayette
Production Artist: Nancy Gustine, B.F.A., Advertising Art, University of North Texas

ISBN: 978-1-57972-928-8
Printed in the United States of America

Table of Contents

A Letter from Chuck

Of all the good guys in the New Testament, there is one who continues to wear the sign of shame—Thomas, the doubter. This isn't Thomas's fault. Theologians and Bible teachers for centuries have never let Thomas live down his moment of misgiving. Too many in my profession have focused too hard on Thomas's "Unless I see . . . I will not believe" statement in John 20:25. They've failed to pay equal attention to his great confession: "My Lord and my God!" (John 20:28).

Yes, Thomas was a doubter, but so were all the disciples. All but John and some women had fled in fear by the time Jesus was crucified. All believed that those women who had seen the empty tomb and reported back to the disciples were crazy. It was only normal for Thomas to doubt. Why? Because it's not normal for dead men to walk out of their graves. And yet, the moment Thomas saw Jesus, doubt instantly turned into belief.

Church tradition tells us Thomas traveled to the most remote parts of the known world. He traveled to India, preaching the truth of Christ's death and resurrection. In fact, it was in India that Thomas was martyred for the faith he no longer doubted.

So I suggest that we remove the sign from Thomas's neck and cut him a little slack. While you're at it, cut yourself some slack too. Every serious follower of Christ experiences times of doubt and questioning. I certainly have. Perhaps you are in the midst of some difficult days of doubt. Maybe you're wondering if God is real, if He hears your prayers, if He cares about you, if He will meet your needs. If so, the volume you hold in your hands will serve as a refreshing oasis in your spiritual desert.

This book will introduce you to two doubters. One will come as no surprise: Thomas. But the other may stop you in your tracks. His name? John the Baptizer. Looking into the spiritual lives of these two men offers the truth that doubters can have a future of great spiritual impact. Giants of the faith are made up of feeble flesh, just like the rest of us.

Wherever you find yourself on your spiritual journey with Jesus—walking in faith or struggling with doubt—the lives of Thomas and John, as well as the practical advice at the end of this book, will encourage you to continue on. I have no doubt that "He who began a good work in you will perfect it until the day of Christ Jesus" (Philippians 1:6).

Journeying with you,

Chuck Swindoll

Charles R. Swindoll

The Anchor

Every soul needs an anchor, for the times are tumultuous. When the gale force winds of life buffet, many begin to doubt. "Is God real?" "Does God care?" "Does God hear my prayers?" Doubt sets the soul adrift.

The cover of this book bears the image of an anchor—an ancient symbol of safety and stability. Since the earliest days of sea exploration, the anchor has been the one sure method of preventing shipwreck. So important was the symbol of the anchor, the writer to the Hebrews used it to encourage his beleaguered readers: "We who have taken refuge [in God] would have strong encouragement to take hold of the hope set before us. This hope we have as an anchor of the soul, a hope both sure and steadfast" (Hebrews 6:18–19). And what is that hope? Christ!

When the storms of doubts come—as surely they will—if we keep our souls tethered to the anchor of hope, hope will set itself fast in Christ until the storms have passed. And in that day, we'll declare with the triumphant Paul, "We've been surrounded and battered by troubles, but we're not demoralized; we're not sure what to do, but we know that God knows what to do; we've been spiritually terrorized, but God hasn't left our side; we've been thrown down, but we haven't broken" (2 Corinthians 4:8–9 MSG).

A Doubter's Prayer

Our Father, encourage us — especially we who often doubt and feel ashamed of our doubt. May we realize that You are in the midst of our reflections and, through such inner searching, we can come to new insights and deeper depths that otherwise we could never have known. . . .

Thank you for accepting us in our struggles and understanding our doubts. . . .

Father, we wish to know You as we've never known You before. May today be the beginning of increasing trust and decreasing doubts.

We ask this in the rock-solid name of Jesus, our Lord and our God.

Amen.

The
BENEFIT *of*
the DOUBT

Encouragement for the Questioning Christian

Growing Beyond Our Doubts
by Charles R. Swindoll

Doubt prompts a broad range of opinions. To a few, doubt represents rank unbelief, the worst kind of blasphemy. To others, doubt exposes the raw side of honesty—that part of you never before seen until it's probed deeply with the penetrating questions of life. It boils down to this: can we have lingering doubts and remain a person of faith? Strong and capable people on both sides disagree.

The great Reformer, Martin Luther, had absolutely no place in his theology for doubt. He scored few things more scathingly than what he termed that "monster of uncertainty," a "gospel of despair." [1] But Alfred Lord Tennyson, on the other hand, wrote:

> There lives more faith in honest doubt,
> Believe me, than in half the creeds. [2]

Down through the centuries, the church has had representatives on both sides. On the one hand, there have always been the Jonathan Edwardses, the George Whitefields, the Dwight L. Moodys, whose strong pulpits have rung with such assurance you would wonder as you read their sermons if they at any time ever entertained a doubt. On the other hand, God has given His church C. S. Lewis, Flannery O'Connor, Blaise Pascal and, more recently, Philip Yancey, who have encouraged us to question.

Is it possible for faith and doubt to coexist? One desperate parent in the New Testament would answer that question with a resounding yes! He's the father of the demon-possessed boy, who in anguish turned to Jesus for help. The father's night had been long and dark as he attempted every imaginable remedy for his son's horror and torture. Nothing worked. The scene that Mark's gospel includes captures, like few others in the Bible, the very real conflict between hope and despair.

> They brought the boy to Him. When he saw Him, immediately the spirit threw him into a convulsion, and falling to the ground, he began rolling around and foaming at the mouth. And He asked his father, "How long has this been happening to him?" And he said, "From childhood. It has often thrown him both into the fire and into the water to destroy him. But if You can do anything, take pity on us and help us!" And Jesus said to him, "'If You can?' All things are possible to him who believes." Immediately the boy's father cried out and said, "I do believe; help my unbelief." (Mark 9:20–24)

When Doubts Emerge

The anguished father watching his son writhe on the ground like a rabid animal strained against the tough stuff of doubt to muster sufficient faith to believe. And this father was bold enough to acknowledge his doubt as well as request Jesus's help to overcome it. I'm so glad God decided to include that candid dialogue in Scripture; aren't you?

You may find yourself occupying a place in the ranks of the doubters of this world. If so, this book was written especially with you in mind. To exacerbate matters, you may live among people who have never once questioned their faith. Their piety makes you feel isolated, even a little weird . . . out of place. Perhaps your doubts have sunk you to the depth of despair. You, too, have cried, "Lord, I believe. Help me in my unbelief."

Daniel Taylor, in his book *The Myth of Certainty*, didn't choose to use the term *doubting Christians*. He referred to the doubters among us as "reflective Christians." Frankly, that works for me. There's not much dignity in doubt, but there is a touch of dignity in reflection. Taylor offered a variety of questions that represent the common struggles of a reflective Christian. Here's a sampling:

- Does one minute it seem perfectly natural and unquestionable that God exists and cares for the world and the next moment uncommonly naive?

- Have you sometimes felt like walking out of a church service because it seemed contrived and empty?

- Someone at work says, "Christians check their brains at the door of the church every Sunday, and most of them don't even bother to pick them up on the way out." Do you find yourself objecting or agreeing?

- How confident are you that you know God's desires regarding the specific political, social, and moral issues which face our society? [3]

According to Daniel Taylor, a non-reflective person asks, "What could be worse than unanswered questions?" In Taylor's view, the reflective person considers *unquestioned answers* his or her struggle. A reflective Christian is one who is thinking deeply, questioning often. When we doubt, our minds are at work.

Taylor went on to explain:

> There is a long tradition of people of faith who have valued and participated in the life of the mind and who have brought their God-given intelligence and imagination to bear on the society in which they have lived. These believers have been involved thoughtfully in their cultures, sometimes as shapers, sometimes as critics, but always as people who thought the human endeavor worthwhile.
>
> But there is also a more troublesome aspect to being reflective. Thinking, as many have discovered, can be dangerous. It can get us in trouble—with others, but also with ourselves. And the suspicion lingers in religious circles that it can also, if we are not very careful, get us in trouble with God.[4]

When are those times I allow my intellect to challenge my beliefs? When do I question? When do I reflect? And candidly, when do I doubt?

Likely, it's at those same crossroads of doubt and faith common to most of us. When we encounter a sudden, unexpected calamity. When we pray for a specific outcome and the exact opposite occurs. When we lose a valued staff member or coworker or when our dearest friend moves away to another state. When we live right and suffer miserably for it. When we take a course at school that makes more sense than what our church believes. Ouch!

When life takes us through unexpected twists and tragic turns, we're often overwhelmed by the tough stuff of doubt.

Thankfully the Bible does not leave us awash in our questions. A familiar story in John's gospel shows us that the answer to much of our doubting is a Person. His name is Jesus and—as He did for one struggling disciple—He helps us in our unbelief . . . transforming those lingering questions into more stabilized faith.

A Reflective Thomas

Remember Doubting Thomas? Of course you do. Talk about a bad rap that stuck! My heart goes out to the poor guy. I'd rather think of him, thanks to Daniel Taylor's analysis, as *Reflective Thomas*. He's the one honest disciple who didn't check his brain at the synagogue door. He had faith in his doubts when his questions weren't answered. He had the guts to question the crowd, to raise his hand and press for answers that made better sense. I call that kind of honesty not only reassuring but valiant. I would love to see the ranks of Christianity filled with more courageous believers willing to declare openly the struggles they have, to weep when they're hurting, to admit their doubts rather than deny them.

In the Shadow of Certain Death

John 11 portrays a raw expression of doubt in the midst of life's tough stuff. Here we meet our man Thomas, his mind engaged and his faith again on the ropes.

Two days after hearing of Lazarus's death, Jesus announced to His disciples that He would be going up to Judea, where Lazarus would certainly be buried. The disciples knew the dangers of going back. Jesus was Public Enemy Number One on Judea's most-wanted list. To complicate things, the religious leaders were already breathing vicious threats against His life.

Not surprisingly, the Twelve attempted to dissuade Jesus from altering His itinerary and walking into harm's way. "Rabbi, the Jews were just now seeking to stone You, and are You going there again?" (John 11:8).

I can't speak for you, but that response makes good sense to me.

Not persuaded, Jesus insisted on returning to Judea, saying, "Lazarus is dead, and I am glad for your sakes that I was not there, so that you may believe; but let us go to him" (11:14–15). At that point something remarkable happened. Reflective Thomas, the one haunted by doubts, spoke up. John wrote, "Therefore Thomas . . . said to his fellow disciples, 'Let us also go, so that we may die with Him" (11:16).

No doubt a chill ran the length of Thomas's spine when he heard Jesus talk of going back to Bethany. But that chill was quickly transformed into iron resolve. Thomas knew the danger and apparently resigned himself to the irreversible decision to follow Jesus, regardless . . . a decision which would eventually cost Thomas his life.

Yet doubt lingers in Thomas's words. As New Testament scholar Merrill Tenney wrote, "His faith was courageous but not triumphant. He was resigned to the possibility of martyrdom as a matter of duty, but he did not entertain the concept of a victory over death and all its powers. Faith had not yet passed from resolution to insight."[5]

All Thomas could envision in the trip to Bethany was certain death. I call that reality. But he didn't know of anybody he'd rather die with than his Master and the other disciples. I call that loyalty.

In the Face of an Uncertain Future

John 14 shows that Thomas had his doubts about the future too. They had come to Jerusalem. It was there Jesus stood in the darkening shadow of the cross. He slipped away to a second-story flat in the busy city where He and the Twelve would gather for their final meal. Jesus had broken the news to them that His death was near. Separation from them was certain. As He scanned the room for their reactions, He read fear and doubt in their eyes. That's when He spoke what were perhaps some of His most tender words as He attempted to calm their worried minds and steel their shaken resolve.

"Do not let your heart be troubled; believe in God, believe also in Me. In My Father's house are many dwelling places; if it were not so, I would have told you; for I go to prepare a place for you. If I go and prepare a place for you, I will come again and receive you to Myself, that where I am, there you may be also. And you know the way where I am going." (John 14:1–4)

Jesus hardly finished His words before Thomas blurted out, "Lord, we do not know where You are going, how do we know the way?" (14:5). I love his unguarded honesty! The rest of the men were thinking the same thing, but only Thomas had the guts to say so. He wasn't arguing, and he wasn't trying to stop the plan. He was stating the truth. He didn't have a clue where Jesus would be going, so Thomas questioned Jesus's comment, ". . . you know the way." The fact is, Thomas didn't know. None of them knew. That's why he asked, "How do we know the way?"

> Jesus said to him, "I am the way, and the truth, and the life; no one comes to the Father but through Me. If you had known Me, you would have known My Father also; from now on you know Him, and have seen Him." (14:6–7)

Now think this through. Had Thomas not expressed his doubts in the form of that question, it's possible Jesus might have never uttered those remarkable words . . . words, in fact, that have brought both hope and comfort to the world since that day. So, good question, Thomas. Good for you.

In the midst of the tough stuff of doubting, Thomas was willing to say, "I don't have this theology wrapped up cleanly in my mind, Jesus. It isn't clear to me. There's something about this heaven talk I can't weave together in my thoughts." Without a hint of rebuke, Jesus graciously worked with Thomas and respected his doubts. He understood his confusion. His fear. His grief.

Truth be told, Thomas's heart was broken. His dreams shattered. His hopes dashed. His plan to hold stock in a triumphant earthly kingdom went belly-up in a single declaration of intent. Not long after that honest interchange between Jesus and His disciples, Thomas watched from a distance as Jesus endured a violent, torturous death. He saw the blood splatter on the road. He saw those thick, iron spikes disappear deep into Christ's hands and feet. He grimaced as the sword pierced His side. Suddenly everything was over. With that, Reflective Thomas went AWOL—vanishing into the shadows of that confusing, depressing day in Jerusalem that had left him a devastated man. He checked out.

Before we go much further, I need to acknowledge that reflective people usually suffer alone. People like Thomas gravitate toward times of solitude and seclusion. I know . . . I'm one of them.

Even the people close to me seldom know those issues I struggle with intensely. Perhaps they shouldn't. But the struggles are there. Now don't misunderstand. I don't doubt my faith in the Lord Jesus. I certainly don't doubt His blood that paid the complete price for my sins, nor do I doubt His resurrection from the grave. But, like Thomas, I have questions. Many of them. My book of learning hasn't been sealed and shipped. My thoughts are still on the presses and they're rolling. The ink's not dry on my journal of questions. I confess to you that it is not uncommon for me in a given week to struggle deeply with things that make me wrestle within and wonder.

When my father died at the age of 87, he had lived with us for four years before we found it necessary to admit him to a very fine, clean place where he lived a while longer. He was kept under the watchful care of my sister and me during his final days in the hospital. I grieved silently. Yet when it came to my duties as a pastor of a growing, dynamic church, it was like someone threw a switch, and I pressed on in my responsibilities.

I preached Dad's funeral to a small gathering of family and friends. I spoke somberly and appropriately about the promises of God and the hope we have beyond the grave. I buried my father's frail body with grace and poise, as all good ministers do. I never missed a beat. I've done that duty hundreds of times throughout my many years in the ministry. I could do much of it with my eyes closed . . . but always with tenderness and compassion.

My sister, Luci, and I got back on the plane to return home. During a quiet moment she asked, "Babe, do you believe every single thing you said today?" It made me think . . . deeply.

"No," I said, almost sighing under my breath. "There are things that the jury's still out on in my mind."

"That's not what I'm asking," she said back to me gently. "I know you believe a lot of it. I just want to know if you fully believe *every single thing*. 'Cause if you do, we're very different."

I said, "No. There are things that I really have a hard time believing and understanding. I just can't fit everything together in my mind and in my heart." She paused, then lovingly put her hand on my arm and with tears in her eyes answered, "That's good, Babe. And that's okay." Perhaps softened by her tender expression of love and honesty, I looked at the clouds outside the window as tears began to flow for my dad and for our losing him.

I fear that too many believers think they have captured the message of Christianity and placed it in a box marked on top, "Don't ask. Don't tell." On the side it reads, "Off limits for doubts and questions."

Does someone in the family need to give you permission to weep when you lose a loved one? I mean, really grieve? Do you feel the freedom to admit, "I just don't know for sure"? Is there a place for you because you're still thinking and still questioning? Bottom line: is it okay to doubt? It's okay! In fact, it is necessary! You must or you won't grow. You'll wind up learning someone else's answers, and in many cases they will be inadequate for your questions . . . if you're honest enough to ask them.

I find airtight conclusions mainly in people who have not hurt much. They're usually people who have become tightly wired, rigid, and isolated from the real world. They're closed . . . unwilling to be vulnerable. Suddenly, a divorce comes. Or someone dies in a tragic set of circumstances or loses his or her job. Reality hits and a storm blows in and threatens their once tranquil existence. The emotional explosion results in more questions than answers. They discover things they didn't really know. They are in the vortex of dilemmas they cannot solve. At that point, simplistic solutions are replaced with realistic reflections . . . and the deep things of God begin to emerge, eclipsing shallow answers.

That explains why Jesus didn't rebuke Thomas and say, "Look in your notebook! We covered that in my discourse on the Mount of Olives—page 59." Instead, Jesus said, in effect, "Thomas, your questions will be settled in Me. I am the way and the truth and the life" (John 14:6).

How could He be "the Way" when they found themselves at a dead end? How could He call Himself "the Truth" when it all appeared to have been a hoax? How could He be "the Life" when they had just been told of His impending death? More unresolved questions lingered in Thomas's fractured soul. For three days after Christ's death, the disciples grieved, haunted by fear, dogged by doubt. But, when Jesus appeared to them, all that changed.

John remembered the transforming encounter:

> So when it was evening on that day, the first
> day of the week, and when the doors were shut
> where the disciples were, for fear of the Jews,

Jesus came and stood in their midst and said to them, "Peace be with you." And when He had said this, He showed them both His hands and His side. The disciples then rejoiced when they saw the Lord. So Jesus said to them again, "Peace be with you; as the Father has sent Me, I also send you." . . . But Thomas, one of the twelve, called Didymus, was not with them when Jesus came. (John 20:19–21, 24)

With hopes dashed and dreams gone, Thomas was nowhere to be found. He was lost in his doubts and disillusionment. Wherever he was, though, the remaining disciples soon found him and exclaimed, "We have seen the Lord!"

But that was not enough for our reflective friend. He wanted tangible proof. That's why Thomas said to them, "Unless I see in His hands the imprint of the nails, and put my finger into the place of the nails, and put my hand into His side, I will not believe" (20:25).

Once again, Thomas owned his doubts. He did not blindly believe because others did. It would take more than a few excited friends to convince him that the horrible events he had witnessed only days before were somehow miraculously reversed. He wanted to touch Jesus's hands, feel the deep imprint of the nail scars, and put his finger in the spear wound in Jesus's side before he would come around. And that is just what Jesus had in mind for Thomas. John wrote of that event too:

> After eight days His disciples were again inside, and Thomas with them. Jesus came, the doors having been shut, and stood in their midst and said, "Peace be with you." Then He said to Thomas, "Reach here with your finger, and see My hands; and reach here your hand and put it into My side; and do not be unbelieving, but believing." Thomas answered and said to Him, "My Lord and my God!"
> (John 20:26–28)

Thomas, having honestly faced his doubts, discovered a firm faith. Once convinced, he yielded.

We get through the tough stuff of doubt the same way—by facing our doubts and bringing them to the Savior! Just like Thomas.

Any question asked without guile is not a skeptical question. It's an honest search. Jesus very graciously responded, "Because you have seen Me, have you believed? Blessed are they who did not see, and yet believed" (20:29).

You're in the "they" of that sentence. "Blessed are you who did not see, and yet believe." Blessed are you, Mary, Doris, Barbara, and Martha. Blessed are you, Bob, Bill, Nathan, and Frank. Blessed are all who haven't seen, yet believe! Blessed are you for bringing your doubts to Him and leaving them at the foot of the cross. It is there—at the cross—where those who can no longer cope with life's doubts are able to work things through. It is the place to which we all must come . . . sooner rather than later.

When You Cannot Cope

May I close this chapter by writing very personally to you? Yes, you. Throughout any life that is lived realistically and reflectively, we come to impossible places where we feel we cannot cope. They may not seem like it, but those are the healthiest places in life . . . and they are also the hardest. When the bottom drops out, when the pain seems unbearable, when some unbelievable event occurs, doubts arrive unannounced. Don't deny them; acknowledge them. Those times of doubting become schoolrooms of learning. As we work our way through them, a new kind of faith is forged. It will come slowly, and that's healthy. It's being shaped on the anvil of God's mysterious plan, some of which you will not be able to explain. And that's okay.

Now the real question is, "How?" How do we grow this new kind of faith in the tough stuff of doubt?

First, *by risking and failing, not always playing it safe.* You can't afford to live a life of fear. You must not always play life safe. Winning over doubts means beginning to live by faith and not by sight. Walking this new journey has its risks. You cannot see around every bend or anticipate every danger. You will sometimes fail, but that isn't fatal!

That's how we grow, by trusting God through the risks we take and the failures we endure. Step out. Refuse to play it safe.

Second, *we keep growing by releasing and losing things valuable, not finding security in the temporal.* At the heart of this technique is the principle of holding all things loosely.

My wife, Cynthia, and I know a couple who have to be as close to the ideal of parents as we've ever met. Every Christmas we get a lovely card from them. For years they were to us the picture-perfect family. Yet one day they found themselves in an inescapable abyss. Their precious daughter was admitted to a psychiatric facility after attempting suicide over an eating disorder. Our dear friends hit absolute bottom. They weren't grinning and quoting verses. They didn't run around smiling at life, quoting tired clichés, like, "In spite of this, God is great; God is good." No, they nearly drowned in their doubts. They wept bitter tears. They questioned everything they ever believed.

Are they still qualified as people of faith though they wavered in the dark? Absolutely. By God's grace, in time, they released those doubts, having faced them honestly, and they refused to seek security in the temporal. Today, looking back, they're convinced those lonely days proved to be some of the best days of their lives. Their walk with the Lord is far more mature than before.

Third, *we continue to grow by questioning and probing the uncertain, not mindlessly embracing the orthodox.* Read that once again, aloud. We don't just blindly swallow someone else's answers. We keep our minds and our hearts engaged in the pursuit of God's truth. By searching Scripture. By seeking God's wisdom and understanding. That's what I mean by questioning and probing.

Fourth, *we grow by admitting and struggling with our humanity, not denying our limitations and hiding our fears.* And I can assure you that this author-for-God understands when you find yourself cornered by doubt. I've been there more times than you'd ever believe. You are definitely not alone.

Perhaps you have just read for the first time in your life that there is room at the cross for your doubts and your questions. Maybe some well-meaning soul has pushed you into a corner and attempted to make you believe or tried to force you into feeling your questions are an offense to Christ. You need to hear anew the tender words of One who knows your doubts and fears better than you. He said, in effect, "Peace be with you. Look at My hands and feet. Look with eyes of faith and believe. You are blessed when you believe in spite of your doubts."

In Defense of a Doubter
by Charles R. Swindoll

An honest doubter is no more a heretic than a questioner is a fool. Are you becoming convinced of that? Let it sink in.

Yes, contrary to popular opinion, some doubting is okay, even healthy. There are times when doubts force us to pursue the truth, when being gullible and believing whatever we are told would lead us into error. Doubts occasionally give us the fuel to pursue questions we have asked for a long time.

I often think of doubts as making us deep-sea divers. They drive us to explore the depths that are dark and often foreboding—to find treasures many people don't even know to look for. Often, those who doubt think more deeply than those who do not. Daniel Taylor in *The Myth of Certainty* noted:

> Reflectiveness, then, is a character trait deeply rooted in what one essentially is. It helps define one's fundamental experience of reality. The life of a reflective person is more likely to be interesting, less likely to be serene; more likely to be contemplative, less likely to be active; more likely to be marked by the pursuit of answers, less by the finding of them. The result is a high potential for creativity, curiosity, and discovery, but also for paralyzing ambivalence, alienation, and melancholy.[1]

Blaise Pascal said, "One must know when it is right to doubt, to affirm, to submit. Anyone who does otherwise does not understand the force of reason." [2]

When Doubt Runs Deep

During our very real periods of doubt, we feel we are in a self-made prison. We are blinded and deafened. Some doubts are so deep they seem devastating. John Bunyan's wonderful allegory, *The Pilgrim's Progress*, illustrates this very example. Christian, the main character, and his friend, Hopeful, fall asleep on the grounds of a place called "Doubting Castle." The castle is owned by Giant Despair, who is married to Diffidence. (I love that name.) Despair finds Christian and Hopeful asleep on his property and takes action.

> The *Giant* therefore drove them before him, and put them into his castle, in a very dark Dungeon, nasty and stinking to the spirit of these two men: Here then they lay from *Wednesday* morning till *Saturday* night, without one bit of bread, or drop of drink, or Light, or any to ask how they did: They were therefore here . . . and were far from Friends and Acquaintance. [3]

That is exactly what happens when you experience doubt. You're without nourishment. You're without light. You're without friendship. You're isolated. People leave you alone. You're cast into the dungeon of your own imagination and fears.

While Christian and Hopeful are in the dungeon, Diffidence leans over in bed one night and convinces Despair to beat them. So, the next morning Despair goes down in the dungeon and beats them. And Christian and Hopeful begin to think about suicide.

If doubts go on long enough and if they're deep enough, you begin to think, *Death is better than this.*

Then, suddenly, a ray of hope shines through.

> Well, on *Saturday* about midnight they began to *pray*, and continued in Prayer till almost break of day.
>
> Now, a little before it was Day, good *Christian*, as one half amazed, [did] break out in this passionate speech: What a Fool, quoth he, am I, thus to lie in a stinking dungeon, when I may as well walk at liberty? I have a key in my bosom, called *Promise*, that will I am persuaded open any lock in *Doubting Castle.* Then said *Hopeful*, that's good news, good brother, pluck it out of thy bosom and try.[4]

Don't you love that? "You've got a key that'll get us out of this dump? Try it! Let's get out!" That's exactly what they do. Christian pulls out the key of Promise, unlocks the door, and he and Hopeful escape the dungeon of doubt.

The same is true of us. In the swirl of our unhappiness and misery, of our fears and imaginations, a promise is made. When we are without friends and without light, a promise is fulfilled. At the very moment we are without nourishment, a promise is remembered. A promise from God's Word. That promise opens the door for us . . . and we're freed.

No one is beyond the weakness of doubt. Not even great doubt. *No one.* Luke 7 includes a case in point. If you can believe it, the one doubting is named John—the one who baptized Jesus.

A Biblical Case in Point: John the Baptizer

John was the son of Elizabeth and Zacharias. He was an unusual boy. I take it that he lost his parents or for some reason was released from them and grew up in isolation and in the harsh realities of the desert. He clothed himself in camel's hair with a leather belt about his waist. He ate, of all things, locusts and wild honey. I mean, this is a weird guy! While he was out in the middle of the wilderness, God began to speak to John. He became the prophetic forerunner who was to prepare the way for the Messiah. What a responsibility! But John didn't go and preach in the silken palaces of the king. He stayed in the wilderness . . . and people came from all around to hear him speak.

John had one message: "Repent, the kingdom of heaven is at hand. I am but a lamp; the Messiah is the Light. I am just a voice; He is the Word. I am His messenger; He is the Message—the Lamb of God who takes away the sins of the world. Repent and follow Him. Turn away from your grave-like lives. All you hypocrites, fall down before God in repentance and prepare yourself for Messiah." That, in effect, was the message of John the Baptizer. A tough message!

When it came time for the messenger and the Messiah to meet eyeball-to-eyeball, Jesus came to the Jordan River to be baptized. John said to Him, "I have need to be baptized by You, and do You come to me?" (Matthew 3:14). But Jesus stood there, waist-deep in the water, and John consented—and baptized Him. The Spirit of God descended like a dove, and the voice of God rang out, "This is My beloved Son, in whom I am well-pleased" (3:17). John the prophet was full of faith as he encountered the Messiah.

But later his faith began to falter, as we read in Luke 7.

> Summoning two of his disciples, John sent them
> to the Lord, saying, "Are You the Expected One,
> or do we look for someone else?" (Luke 7:19)

Can you believe that? This was the same man who announced, "Behold, the Lamb of God" (John 1:29). This was the same man who for months had been preparing the way for Jesus the Messiah. This was the same man who fulfilled Malachi's promise of one who would come with the spirit of Elijah. Now, John questioned the very sermon he preached.

When I first read Luke 7:19, I thought, *Maybe that wasn't what John meant; maybe it wasn't quite like that.* But look at verse 20.

When the men came to [Jesus], they said, "John the Baptist has sent us to You, to ask, 'Are You the Expected One, or do we look for someone else?'"

Essentially, John wanted to know, "Are You Messiah, or have we believed in vain? Should we look for another?" Why would John, a man so full of faith all of his life, at that moment ask Jesus if He was really the Messiah?

Let's think it through. Do you know where John was? He was in prison. Have you ever been in prison? If you have, you know how disillusioning confinement is. You question things you would never otherwise question. Your future is threatened and uncertain. You are at the mercy of the one who holds the key. Even if you have never been in a literal prison with bars, you have likely been in some kind of spiritual prison. Perhaps you have stood behind the bars of a certain sin. Maybe you have struggled with an addiction, a depression, or with the loss of someone very close to you. When those giants of despair grab you, you may find yourself in a prison-like existence. Doubts seem confined with you in your cell. You may even begin to ask, "Have I misunderstood something? Is Jesus really the One?"

F. B. Meyer, one of my favorite authors, wrote these insightful words:

> When first consigned to prison, he [John] had expected every day that Jesus would in some way deliver him. Was He not the opener of

prison-doors? . . . Surely He would not let His faithful follower lie in the despair of that dark dungeon! . . .

But the weeks grew to months, and still no help came. It was inexplicable to John's honest heart, and suggested the fear that he had been mistaken after all. We can sympathize in this also. Often in our lives we have counted on God's interfering to deliver us from some intolerable sorrow. With ears alert, and our heart throbbing with expectancy, we have lain in our prison-cell listening for the first faint footfall of the angel; but the weary hours have passed without bringing him, and we have questioned whether God were mindful of His own.[5]

Jesus Reassures a Doubter

Are You the One, or do we look for another?" John's question was almost as amazing as Jesus's answer. We might expect the Lord to give the instant response: "I'm the One. Go right back, and tell him I'm the One." But Jesus didn't do that. Instead, right on the heels of John's question, Jesus resumed His ministry of healing. He didn't even answer the question . . . at first.

> At that very time He cured many people of
> diseases and afflictions and evil spirits; and He
> gave sight to many who were blind. (Luke 7:21)

Jesus left John's disciples waiting . . . and watching. When Jesus finally answered, He told them, "Go and report to John what you have seen and heard" (7:22). What kind of answer is that?

Why do you think Jesus told them to report to John what they had seen Jesus do and heard Him teach? Because when you're in prison, you can't see or hear what is happening on the outside. Your perception is fogged. Your hearing is muffled. Your world is a world of introspection and a realm of reflection. It's a place of confusion. It's a solar system that orbits around *you*—a world that yearns for freedom and release and answers and relief.

> "Report to John . . . the blind receive sight,
> the lame walk, the lepers are cleansed, and
> the deaf hear, the dead are raised up, the poor
> have the gospel preached to them." (7:22)

What's implied in Jesus's answer is this: "These are the works of Messiah. To be sure, judgment *will come*, but that's later. Tell John I'm right on target."

Just before John's disciples left, however, Jesus added a beatitude— a lesson often forgotten. "Blessed is he who does not take offense at Me" (7:23). A special blessing rests upon those who are trapped in a situation they cannot get out of, when it looks as though the Lord is leaving them and they are being treated unfairly by the world. Blessed are those who live without being offended by Jesus's actions—or lack thereof—in that situation.

The Lord's response was not the answer John's disciples expected. One Bible scholar put his finger on what John probably expected to hear from Jesus, the Messiah:

> "My armies are massing. Caesarea, the head-
> quarters of the Roman government [in Israel],
> is about to fall. The sinners are being obliter-
> ated. And judgment has begun." He would
> have expected Jesus to say, "The wrath of God
> is on the march," but Jesus said, "The mercy of
> God is here." Let us remember that where pain
> is soothed and sorrow turned to joy, where suf-
> fering and death are vanquished, there is the
> kingdom of God. Jesus' answer was, "Go back
> and tell John that the love of God is here."[6]

Do you need that reminder today? In your agenda, is it time for action? Chances are good that's not God's agenda. If it were, there'd be action. If you're swarming with doubts or you know someone who is, it's okay. As a matter of fact, *blessed* are you if you can keep from being offended. Blessed are those who do not view Jesus as a stumbling block. Blessed are the Jobs when their mates suggest, "Curse God and die," and they do not curse. Blessed are the Josephs, who, when people turn against them unfairly, refuse to live lives of bitterness. Blessed are the Hoseas, whose mates walk out on them, though they have been faithful to walk in obedience to God. Blessed are the Pauls, who pray repeatedly, "Lord, take this thorn from me," but to whom God says repeatedly, "No." Blessed are you when you respond, "In weakness I am strong." You believe God's "no" is best, and you are not offended by His reply. Blessed are those who live without offense toward God.

Just a practical word for you with children who have reached that vulnerable period of adolescence and young adulthood. It's cool to be a doubter at college, *so relax.* If your child is experiencing doubts, just remember, he or she is being taught by philosophers. I read somewhere that a philosopher is somebody who talks about things he or she doesn't understand and makes it sound like it's your fault! Your children may try to blow you out of the saddle with questions of doubt. That's okay. Don't panic. They will work through it. Just keep doing what is right and keep standing firm on truth. In time, you'll be amazed by how your kids discover how smart you really are . . . once they learn that their professors don't have all the answers.

Jesus Honors a Doubter

Do you have a John the Baptizer in your family right now—one locked in the prison of doubt? Be very gracious. Be understanding and compassionate, as difficult as it may be. Luke 7:24–29 tells you why. After John's disciples left, Jesus addressed the believing multitudes that stood nearby. The crowd had been listening with their mouths agape, thinking, *John said that? I wonder if we shouldn't have followed John's message? I mean, a man like that—who lived alone in the desert and ate locusts—should we have really believed what he said?*

This was Jesus's moment. If He wanted to rag on John, this was His chance! Few of us would pass up such an opportunity. We may speak in a compassionate manner in the presence of the doubter (or the friends of the doubter), but behind their backs, we mock or criticize them. Jesus didn't do that. Instead, He bragged on John.

Jesus did so with a series of questions: "What did you go out into the wilderness to see?" (Luke 7:24); "What did you go out to see?" (7:25); "What did you go out to see?" (7:26).

Jesus took the multitude back to their earliest recollection of John preaching in the wilderness, before he was behind bars. Jesus reminded them of when they first heard that clarion call in the wilderness. When John spoke of repenting because the kingdom of heaven was at hand. When he pointed to Jesus as the Lamb of God. "What did you go out to see?" Jesus asked—and then He suggested three possible answers.

Did they travel to the wilderness to see "a reed shaken by the wind?" (7:24). In other words, did they expect to see a flimsy little plant easily blown in the breeze—someone who was fickle and vacillating and changing? The answer was clear: *no*—that was not John.

Jesus suggested another possibility: "What did you go out to see? A man dressed in soft clothing? Those who are splendidly clothed and live in luxury are found in royal palaces!" (7:25). Jesus pressed the point, as if to ask: "Did you see some effeminate, thin-skinned weakling, some silk-clad wimp? Or a jester wearing pointed slippers with bells, dancing around to make kings laugh?" Of course not!

The Lord then answered His own question: "What did you go out to see? A prophet? Yes, I say to you, and one who is more than a prophet" (Luke 7:26). Now, how could John have been *more* than a prophet? Either he was one . . . or he wasn't. In those days, prophets were able to predict the future without error. They spoke for God, who makes no miscalculations. John fulfilled a role greater than a prophet because he was the "forerunner . . . in the spirit and power of Elijah" (1:17). John prepared the way for Messiah's coming by preaching a message of repentance (see Malachi 3:1). What tremendous affirmation Jesus gave to John.

Isn't it great news that prophets—and even one "more than a prophet"—can have doubts? That tells us that great men and women of God can still slump into periods where life doesn't fit together.

Jesus didn't stop at simply holding up John as a hero of faith. Jesus went further. "I say to you, among those born of women there is no one greater than John" (Luke 7:28). Wow! Let that sink in. Have you ever read *anywhere* in the Bible of someone receiving that kind of praise from Jesus? No, you haven't. Jesus said that *nobody* in His day was greater. That was John.

No wonder Scripture records the reaction of the multitude to Jesus's endorsement of John.

> When all the people and the tax collectors
> heard this, they acknowledged God's justice,
> having been baptized with the baptism of
> John. (Luke 7:29)

It made sense. Jesus's opinion of John affected the crowd's opinion. Let me add that *your* opinion of someone will affect the opinions that others have about that person. So, be careful with your critical statements. Filter your comments about those experiencing times of doubt. Watch out that you don't tear down their character. They may be going through a temporary slump, and yet God still plans to use them in a powerful way. Never forget: no one is mightily used of God every day of every year of his or her life. This was true of John. This is true of me. This is true of you.

Jesus Cautions Some Doubters

The believing multitude was relieved that the hero of their faith, John, was still counted as faithful in Jesus's eyes. But there's another group Jesus wanted to address—the Pharisees and the lawyers. Lawyers in that day were experts in the Mosaic Law. These word vultures could extract Scripture right down to a gnat's whisker . . . and come up with elaborate lists of legalistic mumbo-jumbo. They were standing on the other side of the crowd, frowning, along with their friends, the Pharisees. Jesus had guts, didn't He? Looking right at "the Pharisees and the lawyers [who] rejected God's purpose for themselves, not having been baptized by John," Jesus said, "to what then shall I compare the men of this generation, and what are they like?" (Luke 7:30–31).

Okay, here it comes! This is great. Jesus drew an analogy of what these unbelievers were like. He said they were like little children:

> "They are like children who sit in the market place and call to one another, and they say, 'We played the flute for you, and you did not dance; we sang a dirge, and you did not weep.' For John the Baptist has come eating no bread and drinking no wine, and you say, 'He has a demon!' The Son of Man has come eating and drinking, and you say, 'Behold, a gluttonous man and a drunkard, a friend of tax collectors and sinners!' Yet wisdom is vindicated by all her children." (7:32–35)

William Hendriksen did a wonderful job describing Jesus's analogy when He referred to children playing in the marketplace.

> We can easily imagine something of this nature happening today. "Let's play wedding," says one child. . . . "Yes, let's do that," say some of the others, and they start whistling a wedding march. But many voices scream back in disgust, "Not that silly stuff. That's not for us." "Then let's play funeral," says the boy who had

been the first to suggest playing wedding. . . . Dolefully the speaker and some others begin to intone a funeral hymn. But their groaning is drowned out by loud protests: "Cut it out. We want none of this sad stuff." So a petty quarrel develops, in which those who had suggested the games are shouting to their playmates, "You're never satisfied. You don't want to play wedding and you don't want to play funeral. What *do* you want to play?" . . .

Jesus, then, is saying, "That is the way you critics are behaving. You are being childish. You are frivolous and are acting irresponsibly, inconsistently. You are never satisfied. You used to be filled with enthusiasm about John; at least, you stood in awe of him and did not find fault with his austerity and call to repentance. But now you say, 'He is too harsh and unsociable; his message is too severe. Why, he must be possessed.' But you are also turning against me, the Son of man. You are pointing the anger at me and saying, 'Though he demands self-denial in others, he himself is a glutton and a drinker, a friend of tax-collectors and sinners. He is too sociable.'" [7]

When I read through this, it reminded me of those who seem to find fault with everything, always criticizing and never landing on any solid beliefs. Their doubts are unproductive. Continuing to find fault and picking at something here or there, they stay away from faith. "John? Too extreme. Jesus? Too sociable. He runs with everybody."

Look at Jesus's ending statement: "Wisdom is vindicated by all her children" (Luke 7:35). In other words, wisdom's children are all those who were wise enough to take to heart the message of John and Jesus. Wisdom vindicates itself. Look at the changed lives. You will not find a perfect one among the ranks of Christians, but you will find change among all of us. God changes those He saves. Perfection awaits us in eternity, but until then, we will stumble and fall. We will even have moments of doubt. And until perfection comes, we rest our case with Him.

Lessons for Doubters

I want to mention three lessons that we can learn from the verses we have studied.

First, *doubting may temporarily disturb, but it does not permanently destroy a relationship with Christ.* John is a wonderful example of this truth. Remember Pascal's words? "One must know when it is right to doubt, to affirm, to submit. Anyone who does otherwise does not understand the force of reason." I'm sure when John's disciples returned with Jesus's message, John submitted. I believe he did not stumble over the actions of Christ.

Second, *special blessings rest upon those who can live with earthly inequities, knowing there are heavenly purposes.* I call this to mind when I get a letter, or when I receive another call, or when I meet someone who tells me something that's happened doesn't seem right. It creates anguish within me, because I'm only seeing it from my tiny view of life. I want to encourage you with the fact that blessings will rest upon you if you don't get offended by those inequities. God has His reasons, which we may never comprehend. But we can trust Him.

Third, *being child*like *is commendable . . . being child*ish *is unacceptable.* Our Lord tells us to come to Him *like* little children (Luke 18:17). It's difficult to be childlike. On the other hand, it's easy to be childish — to be selfish, to be argumentative, to defend ourselves and get our way.

This is a great time for me to ask you a very direct question. Are you a doubting Christian or just a doubter? Perhaps, as we've been discussing this subject, you realize you are the latter. How long are you going to doubt that Jesus died to release you from your prison of sin and that He rose from the dead to release you into a life of new and eternal freedom? You don't have to live in the pit of doubt about that, if you don't want to. The choice is yours.

If you'd like to find out more about Jesus's offer of eternal life, let me encourage you to stop here, turn to page 59, and read about how you can have a relationship with God. Finding the answer to this essential question will lead you to answers to the other questions. It is the first step.

If you're already a believer in Jesus and you're in a time of doubt, it may be the most difficult, melancholy period of your life. May the grace and mercy of God sustain you. As friends walk away from you and as other people talk about you, may God sustain you through this period of doubt. Your doubts are part of your growth.

There is a benefit to the doubt. You can cling to that truth.

Issues and Answers about Doubt

It could be said that Doubt's partner in life is Unbelief, but Doubt's best friend is Questioning. Doubt and Questioning are buddies—neither one leaves the house of faith alone. Whenever we struggle in our faith, Questioning and Doubt are happy to kick us while we're down. No Christian escapes the one-two punch of Questioning and Doubt—all of us have black eyes. But our questions and doubts don't have to defeat us. Answers are available for our questions and assurance is possible for our doubts. The following are some of the most common questions doubting Christians ask. May these practical, biblical responses from Chuck, his trusted colleague Dr. Bryce Klabunde, and his daughter Colleen Swindoll-Thompson serve to strengthen your faith. (You will also find a list of recommended resources at the back of this book.)

How Can I Believe When God Makes No Sense?

I confess to you, at times I doubt God's purpose and promise. When things haven't worked as I thought they would, when I received a no instead of a yes or a yes instead of a no, when I couldn't unravel a situation and fit it with the character of God . . . those have been times when I have said, "I know down inside this isn't right." Sound familiar? To this, the writer of Hebrews comes to us on his knees, saying, "Please, rather than thinking logically, think *theologically*!" That's awfully good advice.

When the bottom drops out of your life, when hope starts to wear thin, when human logic fails to make much sense, think *theologically*! Read Hebrews 6:17–18:

> In the same way God, desiring even more to show to the heirs of the promise the unchangeableness of His purpose, interposed with an oath, so that by two unchangeable things in which it is impossible for God to lie, we who have taken refuge would have strong encouragement to take hold of the hope set before us.

The theological facts are: (1) there is an unchangeable purpose with God; and (2) that purpose is guaranteed with an oath.

It's at this juncture I should add: don't try to explain every detail of God's purpose to someone else. You can't. If you could, you would be God. The only thing you can explain theologically is that it is part of His unchangeable purpose, guaranteed with an oath, neither of which is a lie. That's theological thinking. As Solomon stated so well: "[God] has made everything appropriate in its time" (Ecclesiastes 3:11).

Let me give you a syllogism—a theological syllogism:

> God is in control of the times and seasons.
> Some times are hard and some seasons are dry.
> So the conclusion is:
> God is in control of hard times and dry
> seasons.

We are quick to give God praise when the blessings flow—when the checking account is full and running over; when the job is secure, and a promotion is on the horizon; when the salary is good; when our health is fine. But we have a tough time believing in Him and praising His sovereignty when those things aren't true.

Three Benefits of Thinking Theologically

There are benefits that come from thinking theologically. You'll see three of them right here in these two verses in Hebrews 6. Look again at verse 18:

> So that by two unchangeable things in which it is impossible for God to lie, we who have taken refuge would have strong encouragement to take hold of the hope set before us.

Logical thinking will discourage you; theological thinking will encourage you. That's the first benefit . . . *personal encouragement*. Believe it. You will have "strong encouragement."

The second benefit the Hebrews writer mentioned is a *refuge of hope*. Encouragement is the opposite of discouragement. Hope is the opposite of despair. When you accept the fact that sometimes seasons are dry and times are hard and that God is in control of both, you will discover a sense of divine refuge, because the hope then is in God and not in yourself. That explains why Abraham gave glory to God during the waiting period. "I can't figure it out; I cannot explain it, but Lord, You promised me . . . and I give You glory for this period of waiting, even though I'm getting up in years."

A strong encouragement, a refuge of hope, and for the ultimate benefit, read verse 19:

> This hope we have as an anchor of the soul, a
> hope both sure and steadfast. (Hebrews 6:19)

That's the third benefit . . . *an anchor for the soul.* The word *anchor* is used often in ancient literature, but it is only used once in the New Testament, right here in Hebrews 6. Today, many hymns and gospel songs make use of the anchor metaphor. Every one of them comes back to this verse that refers to the "anchor of the soul."

I distinctly remember when our troop ship arrived (after seventeen days at sea!) at the harbor city of Yokohama, Japan. As we approached the harbor, the skipper stopped our ship and it sat silent in the deep sea, like an enormous, bloated whale. We marines waited on the deck in the hot sunshine as a tiny tugboat left the harbor and came out toward our huge vessel. Soon, a small Japanese gentleman came up the side of our ship and ultimately took the controls of our ship as he personally guided it until we were safely docked in the harbor. Someone later explained the reason to me: there were still mines in the Japanese harbor. (That's a fun thought after seventeen days at sea: "Welcome to Japan; the mines are ready for you!") He guided us through the treacherous waters of the harbor and right up to the pier.

The point of this, of course, is not anchors and skippers, ships and harbors. The point is: what that Japanese gentleman did for us marines is exactly what Jesus Christ does for us, His children, when the bottom of life drops out.

Doubt, you see, will always try to convince you, "You are all alone. No one else knows. Or cares. No one else really can enter in and help you with this." In Hebrews, however, we're assured that Christ is our constant priest — not once a year but forever. He lives in the God-room. He is there, sitting alongside the Father, representing your needs before Him. And, child of God, there is nothing so great for you to endure that Christ does not feel touched by it and stay by you through it.

Some Practical Perspective

When you find yourself dealing with doubt, let me give you three things to remember. First, *God cannot lie*. He can test, and He will; He can say no, and He sometimes will; He can say yes, and He will; He can say "wait," and occasionally He will — but God cannot lie. He must keep His word. Doubt says, "You fool, you're stupid to believe in a God who puts you through this." By faith, keep remembering that God cannot lie.

Here's the second piece of advice that helps me: *we will not lose*. Doubt says, "You lose if you trust God through this. You lose." If I read anything in Hebrews 6, I read that in the mysterious manner of God's own timing, for some unexplainable and yet unchangeable purpose, those of us who trust Him ultimately win — because God ultimately wins.

God cannot lie. We will not lose. Your mate has walked away from you, an unfair departure—you will not lose, child of God. Your baby has been born and for some reason it has been chosen to be one of those special persons on this earth. You will not lose. You've waited and waited, and you were convinced that things in your life would improve, yet things have only gotten worse—keep remembering, you will not lose. God swears on it with an oath that cannot change. You will not lose.

Third—and I guess best of all—*our Lord Jesus does not leave.* To quote a verse from Scripture, He "sticks closer than a brother" (Proverbs 18:24). The writer of Hebrews put it like this:

> Jesus has entered as a forerunner for us, having
> become a high priest forever. (Hebrews 6:20)

That means He is there at any time . . . and always. This hope that Christ can bring, this "anchor of the soul," is the only way through. I have no answer other than Jesus Christ. I can't promise you healing, nor can I predict that your world will come back right side up. But I can promise you that He will receive you as you come in faith to Him. And He will bring back the hope you need so desperately. The good news is this: hope will not only get you through this particular trial, it will ultimately take you into His glorious presence when you die.

—Charles R. Swindoll

Why Doesn't God Answer My Prayer?

Unanswered prayer is one of the most troubling issues Christians face — one we don't talk about much because it shakes us at the very core of our faith.

"Why doesn't God answer my prayer?" The possible reasons can be unsettling, to say the least. "Maybe God doesn't understand how important this is to me." Or more disturbing, "Maybe God doesn't care about me." Worse still, "Maybe God is powerless to help me." Or worst of all, "Maybe God isn't there at all, and I've been praying to the air."

These doubts fly through our minds, and we're afraid to tell anyone about them. Let me reassure you that it's normal to have these thoughts. As Chuck reminded us in chapter 2, even John the Baptizer — who, with his own eyes, had seen the Holy Spirit descend upon Jesus and, with his own ears, had heard God pronounce that Jesus is His Son — wondered whether Jesus was really the Savior.

Take to heart what Jesus told John's disciples: "Go and report to John what you have seen and heard; the blind receive sight, the lame walk, the lepers are cleansed, and the deaf hear, the dead are raised up, the poor have the gospel preached to them" (Luke 7:22). In essence, Jesus told John — and He's telling you — "Yes, I am Messiah, and I'm here; you have not believed in vain."

A season of unanswered prayer may dampen your desire to pray more. You may become afraid to pray, not wanting to get your hopes up and be disappointed again. I can understand your fear. Perhaps I could point out a few principles to guide our prayers in the future.

First, *we must put our hope in the Lord, not in an answer to prayer.* Not realizing it, we might be saying this to God: "Lord, I can only be happy if You give me what I'm asking for." Perhaps by not answering our prayers, the Lord wants to find out whether we can be completely satisfied in Him and not in what He gives us.

Second, *we must stop trying to pray God into a corner; let God be God.* We may not use the following words when we pray, but we may be feeling them: "God, look at all the good things I'm doing for You. Now You owe me something good in return." Or, "God, if You really love me, You'll answer my prayer." Or, "God, I believe You will come through for me. I *really* believe. And because I have such big faith, You need to answer my prayer." Or, "God, I don't ask for much. I just want You to do me this one little favor. Please?" Or, "God, if You answer this one prayer, I'll do anything You say. I promise."

As you can imagine, none of these strategies work very well, and they all almost always lead to disappointment. No matter how hard we try, we can't control God. A better way of praying is to present our requests while acknowledging that God is in control of the results. "God, I place this situation in Your hands. You know my desires. You know my heart. Your will be done."

Finally, *we must be patient and learn to be content with unanswered questions.* Perhaps the most difficult unanswered prayers to accept are our prayers for sick loved ones who have died in spite of our desperate supplications. We wonder, *If God is more powerful than Satan, why doesn't He prevent bad things from happening to His children? Why does He rescue some and not others?* No one knows the answer to these questions, because no one understands completely the mind of God. But we do know this:

> The LORD is righteous in all His ways
> And kind in all His deeds. (Psalm 145:17)

His justice and goodness have already triumphed over evil through the death and resurrection of Christ, and one day, Christ will banish Satan and unleash a flood of blessings that will flow over His faithful followers with unending joy. Can we wait patiently for that day? Can we keep our faith even though loved ones get sick and die for no reason that our hearts can understand?

I know these are difficult things to consider. Your struggles with unanswered prayer may drive you to desire a deeper explanation of God's character, and if so, I urge you to listen to Chuck Swindoll's sermons "Glorying and Groaning" and "Providence Made Practical" from his *Insights on Romans: The Christian's Constitution* series. You can download these messages or order them online at **www.insightworld.org**, or you can request them by calling Insight for Living. (See "Ordering Information" on page 69.) Through your questions, may the Lord guide you to a deeper understanding of Him and a closer walk of faith.

—Bryce Klabunde

45

Why Does My Addiction Deepen My Doubt?

When he doubted the Lord, John the Baptizer was sitting in a dark, lonely dungeon awaiting execution. Perhaps you feel like you are in a dungeon, too—but, in your situation, the chain around your ankle is a compulsive habit or addiction, and the prison cell is built with iron bars of shame, secrecy, and despair.

You thought that Jesus would free you. After all, didn't He come into this sinful world "to proclaim release to the captives . . . to set free those who are oppressed" (Luke 4:18)? But here you are, still chained and doubting Christ's sin-releasing power.

Most people in prison don't want to be there—not really, deep down in their souls—so they expect Jesus to do something *now*. But what if the expectation of *now* is promised to be fulfilled *later*? It's true, Jesus came to set the captives free, and in a spiritual sense, He has done just that. If you have trusted Christ for your salvation, He has rescued you from the eternal penalty of your sin. But only when God ushers you into paradise and rescues you from the power of sin will you be completely free.

Until then, you will still struggle with the flesh—that part of us that desires sin. Jesus has not left you alone in this battle, though. He has sent you the Holy Spirit as your ally in the fight against sin. But one thing you can count on—you will fight this battle in some form or another and to various degrees for the rest of your life.

Jesus didn't promise to take away all our problems. I wish He did! I wish that God would take away my urges to sin so I would never have to fight temptation again. However, if God solved all my problems, I would never grow. I would probably stop depending on Him. My weaknesses, then, become blessings, because they force me to lean heavily on the Lord.

Paul implored the Lord for relief from the thorn he felt in his body, but God kept the pain in place as a constant reminder of Paul's need for divine power. The wounded apostle accepted God's answer and embraced the paradoxical truth of strength through weakness: "And He has said to me, 'My grace is sufficient for you, for power is perfected in weakness.' Most gladly, therefore, I will rather boast about my weaknesses, so that the power of Christ may dwell in me" (2 Corinthians 12:9).

Rather than suffering alone, Paul *boasted* about his weakness and his need for daily grace from heaven. He openly shared his pain with others, and I urge you to talk to a trustworthy Christian about your struggles. James encouraged us to "confess [our] sins to one another, and pray for one another" (James 5:16). You might be surprised to find out how many "church people" have problems similar to yours. I encourage you to find a loving church that understands your struggle with sin and schedule an appointment to meet with a pastor who can connect you with a group for support and care.

Perhaps a worse prison than the cell of sinful habits is the dungeon of denial. We all sin and need God's grace, and yet, not all of us are willing to admit our weaknesses. Jesus said, "It is not those who are healthy who need a physician, but those who are sick; I did not come to call the righteous, but sinners" (Mark 2:17). Jesus bore the judgment for your sin on the cross. If He gave His life for you, then you can be certain that He won't give up on you now! He loves you, and He is there to help as you share your struggles with others and depend on His grace.

—Bryce Klabunde

Lord, Are You Sure?

Recently, my son Jonathan has been asking a particular question after almost everything I say. He asks his question, then follows my answer by asking, "Are you sure?"

"Mom, can I go outside?" "Sure." "Are you sure?" "Yes."

"Mom, can I eat breakfast?" "Absolutely; dive in." "Are you sure?" "I'm sure."

"Mom, can I play X-Box?" "Yep, your chores are done; go right ahead." "Are you sure?" "Yep, I'm sure."

"Mom, can I help you weed?" "YES! (Miracles still happen!) I would love for you to help me weed!" "Are you sure?" "I've never been more sure. Let's get after them!"

For whatever reason, Jon is seeking some reassurance about life. Even some of the basics like eating breakfast and lunch, taking a shower and changing his clothes, going out to play and coming in to rest. He needs to be reminded of my assurance, confidence, and steadfast care over his life.

Have you ever wanted to ask the Lord if He's okay with some of your needs? Have you ever longed to hear Jesus affirm you, your life, your weaknesses, or your wonderings? Having lived with a disabled child for years now, I have asked the Lord more questions than I could count. I've asked for His assurance, His acceptance, and His grace. I've needed to hear that He is absolutely okay with my mistakes, my tears, my fears, my irritations, my failings, and my doubts. When walking through difficult circumstances, we all need to be reminded that our faithful, tender Lord is never disturbed or bothered by us. Never! Never, ever, ever!

So, if you need to be reminded of God's assurance, confidence, and steadfast care over your life, why not talk with Him about it? And if you happen to ask, "Lord, are you sure?" you can know that our great and mighty God is absolutely sure about you, your needs, and your life, and He longs for you to seek His reassurance by asking, "Jesus, are you really, really sure?" Yes, my friend, He is really, really, really sure of you!

If you were to ask Jesus some of the pressing questions on your heart, and He were to answer you today, the conversation might look something like this:

"Lord, are you sure it's okay to cry in front of my kids?"

"Yes, I'm sure."

God tells us in Genesis 2 and 3 that He created life to be enjoyed in perfect harmony, but sin shattered and splintered this perfect gift. Now, each life on earth is encased in an empty, broken cavity . . . lonely, afraid, and in pain. By watching the tears and grief of their parents, children learn how to accept this reality about the world and how to grieve continual loss. Tears purify our longings on earth, they clarify where lasting hope is found, and they testify that grace and mercy are found only in Christ Jesus (1 Peter 5:6–7, 10).

"Lord, are you sure it's okay to make mistakes?"

"Yes, I'm sure."

It's okay to make mistakes. The Lord tells us in His Word that His love for us is unconditional, regardless of our abilities and accomplishments . . . and of our mistakes and failures. Mistakes and failures often reveal areas in our character that need refinement. For example, pride, perfectionism, self-condemnation, and worry often emerge when a mistake or failure surfaces in our lives. Our value to Christ is unconditional; our mistakes can turn a prideful heart into a heart full of humility and compassion (Psalm 51:16–17; James 4:6).

"Lord, are you sure it's okay to question or doubt You?"

"Yes, I'm sure."

Scripture shows us that an unshakable faith is grown through deep and difficult struggles. Our honest doubts and questions are a necessary part of that growth. Bringing them to God allows Him to reveal His unlimited goodness and faithfulness, His unfathomable sovereignty and authority, His unrestrained power and dominion, and His unimaginable grace and mercy. His immeasurable blessings are provided in abundance as we question, doubt, and learn to trust Him, even though we may never understand or know why (Job 23:1–13).

"Lord, are you sure it's okay to be weak and powerless?"

"Yes, I'm sure."

In His Word, God promises that when we are weak, He will fill us with His strength. When we are unable, God promises to make a way; when we are stricken with grief, God promises His comfort; and when we are powerless, God assures us of His abundant might (2 Corinthians 12:9–10).

"Lord, are you sure it's okay to feel angry, afraid, or upset?"

"Yes, I'm sure."

The book of Psalms is a poignant depiction of people pouring out their honest emotions before a God who listens, hears, and accepts. Emotions and feelings speak about what's happening in our hearts. Our spiritual growth often depends on acknowledging what we feel and learning the way of wisdom despite what emotions and feelings pass through us (Psalm 19:7–14; 46:1–11).

"Lord, are you sure it's okay to rest and take time for myself, even if there are unlimited unmet needs?"

"Yes, I'm sure."

God's Word tells us He has prepared green pastures and quiet brooks where we can find refreshment. In rest, distractions are removed and our souls are restored. By slowing down, we allow God to lead and guide us in all our ways. In rest, we surrender to God's ways and allow Him to carry our burdens (Psalm 23; Matthew 11:28–30).

"Lord, are you sure it's okay to miss church sometimes?"

"Yes, I'm sure."

God's Word assures us that corporate worship is one of many disciplines God's children need. We can allow His wisdom to direct us through the Holy Spirit and His Word, rather than being tied to the rules of humankind. The discipline of worship is not limited to a few hours in our week; worship is meant to be a continual lifestyle. Therefore, we will need to make room for worshiping with others and times for worshiping alone (Psalm 1; John 4:19–24; Romans 12:1–3; Hebrews 10:24–25).

Still wondering if it's okay to ask these questions?

When my son asks, "Mom, are you sure?" I take in my hands his little face with his wondering eyes, his listening ears, and his look of doubt, and I say, "Yes, Jon, I am sure."

To you, my friend, Jesus holds out His hands and says, "Yes, my child, I am here, and I am sure."

—Colleen Swindoll-Thompson

Does Doubting Mean I'm Not Saved?

When we trust Christ for our salvation, God forgives, redeems, justifies, and seals us. He does all the work! As Chuck Swindoll sometimes says, "Salvation is not a do-it-yourself kit; it's a don't-do-it-yourself kit!" Because we don't earn our salvation, we can't lose it. It comes to us as a free gift to keep forever.

All we must do is receive the gift. Paul said it plainly: "For by grace you have been saved through faith; and that not of yourselves, it is *the gift of God*; not as a result of works, so that no one may boast" (Ephesians 2:8–9, emphasis added). This is an important point to understand with regard not only to our salvation but also our security in it. Because we don't have to work to *get* our salvation, we don't have to work to *keep* it. Our salvation and our security depend entirely on Christ.

Let me offer an illustration that helps me grasp this concept. When you board an airplane, you don't have to worry whether or not you have the skills to operate the plane. You just have to get on the plane; that's all the faith you need. The pilot and the plane take you to your destination. The same is true for our salvation. All we must do is trust Christ, and He takes us to heaven.

Many Christians worry that they don't have the right kind of faith to be saved or that they might lose their salvation if they sin—as if their salvation depended on them. In a sense, they've climbed onto the wing and are frantically flapping their arms because they're afraid the plane won't work without their help. If that is true for you, I encourage you to rest in Christ, who is at the controls and who is winging you toward your celestial home. The apostle Paul summed it up this way:

> For I am not ashamed of the gospel, for *it is the power of God for salvation* to everyone who believes, to the Jew first and also to the Greek. (Romans 1:16, emphasis added)

Now, let's address a couple of related questions that many Christians wonder about. *If salvation is a gift from God, then how do we know that we have the gift?* You can know that you have the gift if you have received it. God gives everyone a choice to trust in Jesus for their salvation or to trust in themselves and their good deeds. When you decide to trust Jesus, you move from unbelief to belief, and you have the gift of salvation not because you feel saved but because the Bible says you are.

Is it possible for a believer to have doubts? The answer is yes. Every believer wonders sometimes whether or not God is real and the Bible is true. Let me reassure you that it's normal to have these thoughts. Even some of the most godly people in the Bible struggled with doubts. We've looked at two of them closely in this book—John the Baptizer and Thomas the disciple.

Was John an "unbeliever" because he doubted? No, he was still a believer. Was Thomas an "unbeliever" because he doubted? Of course not. Remember, he's the one who made that great confession: "My Lord and my God!" (John 20:28). They still had faith, but their faith was tested in the furnace of doubt. God sometimes uses our doubts to strengthen our faith, like a blacksmith uses fire to forge steel.

Doubting doesn't mean you have stopped believing; it simply means you are questioning what you believe—and the answers are at your fingertips in God's Word! As you wrestle with the questions and discover solid answers in the Bible, your faith—and assurance—will grow.

—Bryce Klabunde

Endnotes

A Doubter's Prayer

Adapted from *The Prayers of Charles R. Swindoll: Devotional Prayers on 31 Themes*, vol. 1 (Plano, Tex.: IFL Publishing House, 2010), 6–7.

Growing Beyond Our Doubts

Excerpted from Charles R. Swindoll, "Getting Through the Tough Stuff of Doubt," in *Getting Through the Tough Stuff: It's Always Something!* (Nashville: W Publishing, 2004), 61–74. Reprinted by permission of Thomas Nelson Inc., Nashville, Tennessee. All rights reserved.

1. Edward M. Plass, comp., *What Luther Says: An Anthology* (St. Louis: Concordia, 1972), 426.

2. Alfred Tennyson, "In Memoriam," in *Baker's Pocket Treasury of Religious Verse*, Donald T. Kauffman, comp. (Grand Rapids: Baker Book House, 1962), 174.

3. Daniel Taylor, *The Myth of Certainty* (Downers Grove, Ill.: InterVarsity, subsidiary rights owned by Daniel Taylor, 1986), 14–15.

4. Taylor, *The Myth of Certainty*, 16.

5. Merrill C. Tenney, *John: The Gospel of Belief, An Analytic Study of the Text* (Grand Rapids: Eerdmans, 1948), 173.

In Defense of a Doubter

Adapted from Charles R. Swindoll, "In Defense of a Doubter," in *The Continuation of Something Great,* message series (1992).

1. Daniel Taylor, *The Myth of Certainty: The Reflective Christian and the Risk of Commitment* (Waco, Tex.: Word Books, 1986), 18.

2. Blaise Pascal, *Pensées*, #170, trans. A. J. Krailsheimer (New York: Penguin, 1995), 53.

3. John Bunyan, *The Pilgrim's Progress: From This World to That Which Is to Come* (Westwood, N.J.: Barbour, 1985), 129.

4. Bunyan, *The Pilgrim's Progress*, 134.

5. F. B. Meyer, *John the Baptist* (New York: Fleming H. Revell, 1900), 148–49.

6. William Barclay, *The Gospel of Luke*, The New Daily Study Bible (Louisville: Westminster John Knox Press, 2001), 107.

7. William Hendriksen, *New Testament Commentary: Exposition of the Gospel According to Luke* (Grand Rapids: Baker Book House, 1978), 400–401.

Issues and Answers about Doubt

Article "How Can I Believe When God Makes No Sense?" adapted from Charles R. Swindoll, *Hope: Expect Great Things from God* (Plano, Tex.: IFL Publishing House, 2006), 18–30.

How to Begin a Relationship with God

Doubts are one of the most frightening aspects of the spiritual life. Doubts set the soul adrift on an empty sea. Without a rudder or a star to steer by and without an anchor to keep it from the shoals, the doubting soul is at risk of being given over to an aimless and tumultuous belief system. Though frightening, doubts can also become the one key motivator propelling a soul toward safe harbor and away from eternal shipwreck.

If you are one who suspects there must be more to life than it seems, who questions the existence of God or wonders whether there really is such a thing as eternal life, then the Bible can be your reliable navigational chart. It marks the path to finding answers by first marking the path to a relationship with God, beginning with four essential truths.

Our Spiritual Condition: Totally Depraved

The first truth is rather personal. One look in the mirror of Scripture, and our human condition becomes painfully clear:

"There is none righteous, not even one;
There is none who understands,
There is none who seeks for God;
All have turned aside, together they have become useless;

There is none who does good,

There is not even one." (Romans 3:10–12)

We are all sinners through and through—totally depraved. Now, that doesn't mean we've committed every atrocity known to humankind. We're not as *bad* as we can be, just as *bad off* as we can be. Sin colors all our thoughts, motives, words, and actions.

If you've been around a while, you likely already believe it. Look around. Everything around us bears the smudge marks of our sinful nature. Despite our best efforts to create a perfect world, crime statistics continue to soar, divorce rates keep climbing, and families keep crumbling.

Something has gone terribly wrong in our society and in ourselves—something deadly. Contrary to how the world would repackage it, "me-first" living doesn't equal rugged individuality and freedom; it equals death. As Paul said in his letter to the Romans, "The wages of sin is death" (Romans 6:23)—our spiritual and physical death that comes from God's righteous judgment of our sin, along with all of the emotional and practical effects of this separation that we experience on a daily basis. This brings us to the second marker: God's character.

God's Character: Infinitely Holy

How can God judge us for a sinful state we were born into? Our total depravity is only half the answer. The other half is God's infinite holiness.

The fact that we know things are not as they should be points us to a standard of goodness beyond ourselves. Our sense of injustice in life on this side of eternity implies a perfect standard of justice beyond our reality. That standard and source is God Himself. And God's standard of holiness contrasts starkly with our sinful condition.

Scripture says that "God is Light, and in Him there is no darkness at all" (1 John 1:5). God is absolutely holy—which creates a problem for us. If He is so pure, how can we who are so impure relate to Him?

Perhaps we could try being better people, try to tilt the balance in favor of our good deeds, or seek out methods for self-improvement. Throughout history, people have attempted to live up to God's standard by keeping the Ten Commandments or living by their own code of ethics. Unfortunately, no one can come close to satisfying the demands of God's law. Romans 3:20 says, "By the works of the Law no flesh will be justified in His sight; for through the Law comes the knowledge of sin."

Our Need: A Substitute

So here we are, sinners by nature and sinners by choice, trying to pull ourselves up by our own bootstraps to attain a relationship with our holy Creator. But every time we try, we fall flat on our faces. We can't live a good enough life to make up for our sin, because God's standard isn't "good enough"—it's *perfection*. And we can't make amends for the offense our sin has created without dying for it.

Who can get us out of this mess?

If someone could live perfectly, honoring God's law, and would bear sin's death penalty for us—in our place—then we would be saved from our predicament. But is there such a person? Thankfully, yes!

Meet your substitute—*Jesus Christ*. He is the One who took death's place for you!

> [God] made [Jesus Christ] who knew no sin to be sin on our behalf, so that we might become the righteousness of God in Him. (2 Corinthians 5:21)

God's Provision: A Savior

God rescued us by sending His Son, Jesus, to die on the cross for our sins (1 John 4:9–10). Jesus was fully human and fully divine (John 1:1, 18), a truth that ensures His understanding of our weaknesses, His power to forgive, and His ability to bridge the gap between God and us (Romans 5:6–11). In short, we are "justified as a gift by His grace through the redemption which is in Christ Jesus" (Romans 3:24). Two words in this verse bear further explanation: *justified* and *redemption*.

Justification is God's act of mercy, in which He declares righteous the believing sinners while we are still in our sinning state. Justification doesn't mean that God *makes* us righteous, so that we never sin again, rather that He *declares* us righteous—much like a judge pardons a guilty criminal. Because Jesus took our sin upon Himself and suffered our judgment on the cross, God forgives our debt and proclaims us PARDONED.

Redemption is Christ's act of paying the complete price to release us from sin's bondage. God sent His Son to bear His wrath for all of our sins—past, present, and future (Romans 3:24–26; 2 Corinthians 5:21). In humble obedience, Christ willingly endured the shame of the cross for our sake (Mark 10:45; Romans 5:6–8; Philippians 2:8). Christ's death satisfied God's righteous demands. He no longer holds our sins against us, because His own Son paid the penalty for them. We are freed from the slave market of sin, never to be enslaved again!

Placing Your Faith in Christ

These four truths describe how God has provided a way to Himself through Jesus Christ. Because the price has been paid in full by God, we must respond to His free gift of eternal life in total faith and confidence in Him to save us. We must step forward into the relationship with God that He has prepared for us—not by doing good works or by being a good person, but by coming to Him just as we are and accepting His justification and redemption by faith.

> For by grace you have been saved through faith; and that not of yourselves, it is the gift of God; not as a result of works, so that no one may boast. (Ephesians 2:8–9)

63

We accept God's gift of salvation simply by placing our faith in Christ alone for the forgiveness of our sins. Would you like to enter a relationship with your Creator by trusting in Christ as your Savior? If so, here's a simple prayer you can use to express your faith:

Dear God,

I know that my sin has put a barrier between You and me. Thank You for sending Your Son, Jesus, to die in my place. I trust in Jesus alone to forgive my sins, and I accept His gift of eternal life. I ask Jesus to be my personal Savior and the Lord of my life. Thank You. In Jesus's name, amen.

If you've prayed this prayer or one like it and you wish to find out more about knowing God and His plan for you in the Bible, contact us at Insight for Living. Our contact information is on the following pages.

We Are Here for You

If you desire to find out more about knowing God and His plan for you in the Bible, contact us. Insight for Living provides staff pastors who are available for free written correspondence or phone consultation. These seminary-trained and seasoned counselors have years of experience and are well-qualified guides for your spiritual journey.

Please feel welcome to contact your regional Pastoral Ministries by using the information below:

United States
Insight for Living
Pastoral Ministries
Post Office Box 269000
Plano, Texas 75026-9000
USA
972-473-5097
Monday through Friday,
8:00 a.m.–5:00 p.m. central time
www.insight.org/contactapastor

Canada
Insight for Living Canada
Pastoral Ministries
PO Box 8 Stn A
Abbotsford BC V2T 6Z4
CANADA
1-800-663-7639
info@insightforliving.ca

Australia, New Zealand, and South Pacific
Insight for Living Australia
Pastoral Care
Post Office Box 443
Boronia, VIC 3155
AUSTRALIA
1300 467 444

United Kingdom and Europe
Insight for Living United Kingdom
Pastoral Care
PO Box 553
Dorking
RH4 9EU
UNITED KINGDOM
0800 915 9364
+44 (0)1306 640156
pastoralcare@insightforliving.org.uk

Resources for Probing Further

Doubters are questioners. And questioners want answers. Though answers are not always available, hope is. If you find yourself in the depths of doubt, the following resources will help point you to the source of hope — Jesus — and just might provide some answers to your questions. But keep in mind, we cannot always endorse everything a writer or ministry says in these works, so we encourage you to approach these and all other nonbiblical resources with wisdom and discernment.

Guthrie, Nancy. *Holding On to Hope: A Pathway through Suffering to the Heart of God*. Wheaton, Ill.: Tyndale House, 2002.

Insight for Living. *Hope for Our Troubled Times*. Plano, Tex.: IFL Publishing House, 2009.

Swindoll, Charles R. *Getting Through the Tough Stuff: It's Always Something*. Nashville: Thomas Nelson, 2006.

Swindoll, Charles R. *Hope Again: When Life Hurts and Dreams Fade*. Nashville: W Publishing, 1996.

Swindoll, Charles R. *The Grace Awakening*. Nashville: Thomas Nelson, 2010.

Yancey, Philip. *Disappointment with God: Three Questions No One Asks Aloud*. Grand Rapids: Zondervan, 1992.

Yancey, Philip. *Where Is God When It Hurts?* Grand Rapids: Zondervan, 1990.

Ordering Information

If you would like to order additional copies of *The Benefit of the Doubt: Encouragement for the Questioning Christian* or order other Insight for Living resources, please contact the office that serves you.

United States

Insight for Living
Post Office Box 269000
Plano, Texas 75026-9000
USA
1-800-772-8888
Monday through Friday,
7:00 a.m.–7:00 p.m. central time
www.insight.org
www.insightworld.org

Canada

Insight for Living Canada
PO Box 8 Stn A
Abbotsford BC V2T 6Z4
CANADA
1-800-663-7639
www.insightforliving.ca

Australia, New Zealand, and South Pacific

Insight for Living Australia
Post Office Box 443
Boronia, VIC 3155
AUSTRALIA
1300 467 444
www.insight.asn.au

United Kingdom and Europe

Insight for Living United Kingdom
PO Box 553
Dorking
RH4 9EU
UNITED KINGDOM
0800 915 9364
www.insightforliving.org.uk

Other International Locations

International constituents may contact the U.S. office through our Web site (www.insightworld.org), mail queries, or by calling +1-972-473-5136.

About the Writers

Charles R. Swindoll

Charles R. Swindoll has devoted his life to the clear, practical teaching and application of God's Word and His grace. A pastor at heart, Chuck has served as senior pastor to congregations in Texas, Massachusetts, and California. He currently pastors Stonebriar Community Church in Frisco, Texas, but Chuck's listening audience extends far beyond a local church body. As a leading program in Christian broadcasting, *Insight for Living* airs in major Christian radio markets around the world, reaching people groups in languages they can understand. Chuck's extensive writing ministry has also served the body of Christ worldwide, and his leadership as president and now chancellor of Dallas Theological Seminary has helped prepare and equip a new generation for ministry. Chuck and Cynthia, his partner in life and ministry, have four grown children and ten grandchildren.

Bryce Klabunde

Bryce Klabunde has been a member of the Insight for Living team as a writer and pastor since 1991. His credits include degrees in Bible exposition (Dallas Theological Seminary, master of theology, 1987) and pastoral care and counseling (Western Seminary, doctor of ministry,

2006). Currently, he serves Insight for Living part-time as historian and content consultant. His full-time ministry is at College Avenue Baptist Church in San Diego as soul care pastor, overseeing the care and counseling ministries. At the center of his life are his wife, Jolene; his four children; and his calling—to help hurting people with the healing principles of God's Word.

Colleen Swindoll-Thompson

Colleen Swindoll-Thompson serves as director of Special Needs Ministries at Insight for Living. She is a graduate of Trinity University with a degree in communication and a double-minor in psychology and education. Colleen continues to pursue a master's degree at Dallas Theological Seminary. As the mother of three children—the youngest of whom has multiple, complex disabilities—Colleen's passion is to provide truth, practical support, guidance, and encouragement to both those who suffer with special needs and those who care for people with special needs.